Activate your Home or Office

For Success and Money

With Feng Shui

Copyright © 2016 Termina Feng Shui. All rights reserved. No part of this book may be reproduced or transmitted in any form without written permission from the authors and publisher, except for brief inclusion of quotations or for review purposes. First Edition

This book is designed to provide competent and reliable information regarding the subject matter covered. However, it is sold with the understanding that the author and publisher are not engaged in rendering legal, financial, or other professional advice. Laws vary from country to country and if legal or other assistance is required, the services of a professional should be sought. The intent of the author is only to offer information of a general nature to help you in your quest for well-being, the author and the publisher assume no responsibility for your actions. The author shall have no liability or responsibility to any person or entity regarding physical, psychological, emotional, financial, commercial damages, special, incidental, or consequential by the information contained in this book.

Contents

Introduction
What is Feng Shui
Invite your fortune in
Clutter management
Activate your wealth zone
- Abundance
- Power and Career
- Fame and Recognition
- General Supportive Luck
- The Trinity of Luck
- General Collaboration
- Enhance Your Connection to Heaven
- Business Collaboration
- Education Collaboration

Areas in the environment
- Lounge and Family Room
- Dining Room
- Bedroom
- Bathroom and Kitchen
- Front Door
- Workspace/Office
- Outside Areas
- Cleansing
- Express Happiness
- General

Wealth enhancers
- Clarity
- Celebration
- Honesty and Honour
- Purity
- Joy
- Transparency
- Faith

- Transformation
- Focus
- Compassion
- Empowerment/Self-Empowerment
- Magnificence
- Balance

Quick tips
Create a vision Board
The power of You

Introduction

I'll start this with a brief story:

The two sat on the veranda, lounged on deck chairs, wiping the sweat from their necks and staring at the stillness before them. The day was too hot, where was everyone? Inside? The humming of air conditioners and the sound of a whimpering dog was all that could be heard.

The visitor sipped his ice filled lemonade and paused to look at the dog that lay less than a metre away, his eyes full of sadness and his head supported by both paws.

"Why is he whining?" he asked the host who was the owner of this dog.

"Because he is laying on a nail,' was the reply.

"Well, why doesn't he move?"

The owner looked at his dog, sipped once from his own lemonade and replied,

"Because it doesn't hurt enough."

Whether it be our relationships, health, finances or personal growth, many do not change their situation even though it hurts and though these experiences come in different shapes and sizes there are similar patterns and we ask ourselves, why me? Why do I always pick the wrong person, why can't I feel better, why can't I be rich?

The question to ask yourself is:

- Why wait until it hurts too much!
- What do I want?
- Why do I have the same patterns?
- What is success to me?
- What is wellness for me?
- What does personal growth mean to me?
- What kind of family, work and friendship relationships make me happy?
- What do I really want?
- How do I make this happen?

The important thing to remember is that your environment is your physical visualisation board and this unconsciously creates your outcomes, 24 hours a day, 7 days a week. The Chinese and now quantum physics teach us that we are surrounded by energy, in fact, everything is energy. Our environment is energy. Einstein told us this *"Everything is energy and that's all there is to it. Match the frequency of the reality you want and you cannot help but get that reality. It can be no other way. This is not philosophy. This is physics."* Energy or energy forces in Feng Shui are termed as Qi (chi). A good flow energy, also known as frequency, leads to abundance, prosperity and happiness while negative energy leads to misfortune and unhappiness.

What do you want? Is it good health? The importance of wellness is imperative. Without good health many areas in our life do not function well, nor can we achieve our fullest potential. However, without necessities, comforts and money to buy good food, warm clothing, pay for the heating bill, or the services that can help with wellness it is futile to focus purely on our health. Through lack and concerns with no money or resources we worry, stress and even conflict with our loved ones. This amplifies poor health and this cycle returns again and again in varied ailments. Therefore, it is imperative to improve your financial wealth as well as your success to live the life with a positive flow of energy.

Feng Shui principles work in harmony with the direct relationship between your success and wealth, through the quality of energy in your home or workplace and opens the flow of Qi for the prosperity and abundance you desire in your life.

Whether you are Building, Designing, Buying, Renting, Selling, Living or Working in a premises, Feng Shui improves your life in so many ways. If there is something going on in your life that you wish to change or improve: Health, career, relationships, financial issues, support, business, wealth, or academic achievement. — You name it — it's all possible by adjusting your environment. All of life circumstances fall under the Feng Shui umbrella of possibilities and there is no limit to what you can improve or amplify positively when these ancient principles and science is applied. Through the art and science of Feng Shui we can improve different aspects of life in areas such as:

Environment psychology
Physical spaces influence the way we feel, think, and interact with the world, it is our auto pilot for outcomes. Feng Shui principles contain activations and cures to improve our quality, happiness and success in life.

Architecture and Design
Feng Shui contributes to all kinds of building-related projects and is increasingly sought after and valued in a broad span of projects involving interior design, lighting design, garden and landscape design, urban design, master planning, property renovation, construction and architecture.

Success

Through environmental psychology and personal preferences, Feng Shui practices activate and enhance success by inviting more flow in money, work or acknowledgement.

Growth

Whether it is Educational, spiritual, or personal advancement Feng Shui practice activates and enhances the Qi flow.

Health and Wellbeing

Feng Shui helps create and maintain good health through connection with the environment and how a person feels and functions in their environment. Enhancing health includes clutter management, space cleansing and environmental psychology.

Clutter management

Letting go of things that have negative connections or serve no worthwhile purpose. This makes space for positive replacements. Feng Shui recognises that clutter can make people feel disorganised, uncreative, tired, anxious and burdened. It is a fundamental Feng Shui principle to physically remove clutter, reorganise storage and clear obstructed spaces.

Feng Shui Space cleansing

Energy can neither be created nor *destroyed*; rather, it transforms from one form to another. Space cleansing the environment transforms the energy and can leave a clearer, lighter and happier atmosphere.

With Feng Shui we can arrange our environment so that we receive maximum support with solutions for improvement, maximising the energy of the home or office for the occupants so that there is improvement in the health, wealth and relationship areas of their lives. The 4000-year-old art and science of Feng Shui helps harness the power of good energy in the home and cures the effects of negative energy. Many home and business owners confirm to the fact that Feng Shui has helped them with their struggles, increased their success and even result in a more attractive living or work space.

What is Feng Shui

Feng Shui is a science and ancient art based on laws that govern the flow of energy. The term Feng Shui translates to "wind-water" in English and is a Chinese Metaphysic Art, practised through formulas and calculations using energy forces referred to as Qi (chi). Both Feng and Shui are associated with good health and prosperity which is why the art is so highly regarded in the east. Energy in the environment remains stuck, people are prevented from moving forward, or experience unwanted circumstances, however, by increasing the flow of energy this clears the path to propel forward and to bring to fruition desired intentions. By creating Positive changes in the environment, it produces improvements in the level and flow of Qi energy bringing high levels of good fortune and creating a more favourable and harmonious layout for a home or office.

Today Feng Shui is used widely around the world, seeing value in what the Chinese have known for years and the objectives vary depending on the home or business owners desired outcome. The common desired outcomes include; healthy family relationships, improved physical and mental health, preservation or growth of financial wealth and harmony. When we consider the energy, we put out and take in, and apply the

Feng Shui principles, we discover that we have more control over our lives than we originally believed. Feng Shui is our opportunity to direct the flow of energy in our lives as we choose. For those of you looking for a way to bring more success into your life, you can use the basics of Feng Shui to help you achieve your goal.

This book contains tips provided in a manner through harnessing the positive energies that you and your property can receive through the use of Feng Shui principles.

Activate your Home or Office For Success and Money

Invite your fortune in

Feng Shui is a science that works beyond the physical world of cause and effect, operating on an energetic level to bring you the highest levels of good fortune. Using Feng Shui principles you create a better flow of energy in your environment and consciously direct that flow to achieve what you desire in your life.

The positive energy of an environment surrounds you and influences you 24 hours a day, seven days a week, your whole lifetime, this also applies to uncured negative energy. Feng Shui is like a form of acupuncture or bar codes for the unified field of energy that includes your home and body. Activate or cure areas within your home or workspace and you start a flow of energy through your body, mind, and soul for more success in your career, health, relationships and growth.

Brain Waves - Your home or workspace is a living, vibrating energy in a vast unified field of energy. Everything in a home influences the flow of active and passive energy also known as positive or negative Qi. This energy wave of flow is similar to the brainwaves formed from your own thinking process. The outcomes in your life are results of brain waves you habitually create with your thoughts. And the outcomes you experience in life are either suppressed or enhanced by the energy fields or environmental brainwaves emitting in your physical surroundings.

There are two brainwave energy fields or environmental brainwaves are beta and alpha frequencies. Beta frequencies reflect chaos and are present in cluttered rooms, drab, dirty spaces, environments with no cosiness or spaces filled with depressing or violent images, dead flowers and piles of papers. This environment feels overwhelming and joyless. It produces victim mentality where one feels unsupported. It creates the feeling of struggling uphill. In this state it is very hard to create what you want toward a better life. However, when you begin to declutter and clean the spaces. Introduce colours and uplifting images, the beta energy wave's shift to bring in the flow of alpha brainwaves. You invite in new opportunities and attract more of the power available to you. This positive flow brings to you good fortune in your career, relationships, health and growth as well as feeling more empowered.

Feng Shui has shown through the centuries that improving your fortune is within your control. When you change or add other things such as colours or items or position your furniture such as your desk or bed in your surroundings, this creates a positive spiralling of energy upward that affects your good fortune and you are in a much better position to attract what you desire. When you decide what you want or to make a change in your life the first thing you must do is get rid of the old to make room for the new.

If you want prosperity, you must make room and invite it in. Before building the structure of prosperity or the money and success energy, you must first lay the foundation, much like a building, without the right foundation the building cannot withstand its longevity and will have complications in some areas where it may lean or sink. If you don't move the rubble and rocks from where the foundations are being placed you will have short, deep and crooked stumps, and a building that is out of whack. Your foundational work is to ensure your home or workplace is free of clutter.

Start with your entry point also known as the mouth of Qi, and this includes your front door. It is the energy connection of your home. It is where the Qi enters along with what you and others bring or take with you. When you leave, you take what you're feeling with you into your day. When you come home, you bring in all that has happened to you throughout the day.

The first priority for your mouth of Qi is to clear the clutter from around your door. If you and your family store shoes, coats, equipment, toys, or any other items by the front door, move them. The clutter blocks the free flow of energy, and it prevents abundance from entering your life.

By placing items and images you activate environmental affirmations that represent what it is you want to have happen in this area of your life. These environmental affirmations are your physical visualisation board. Every time you look at your items or objects you are sending the Qi in this direction, consciously and unconsciously.

Front Door

To increase and enhance your income:

- Entry should be clean and unobstructed.
- Place shoes in a closet or enclosed area. Everything must have its place
- Ensure the door opens easily and quietly. Oil any squeaky hinges

- Clean the glass, if door has glass and windows at entrance
- Paint the door if it is worn, faded or paint peeling.
- In the Chinese culture, three Chinese coins tied together with a red ribbon signifies wealth. Once the front area is clean, you can hang this from your door handle. Tie the coins on the inside and visualise the money flowing into your house every time you open your door. You can usually find these in Asian grocery stores or online.
- You can also place an image or item of a three-legged frog with a coin in its mouth to attract wealth. The best place for your frog is diagonal from the front door and under a table.
- Ensure the entryway is well-lit. Natural light is best, so keep the blinds or curtains open during the day, lamps help also.
- Put out a new welcome mat every year. Door mats should not have holes, this signifies gaps in your prosperity.
- Remove images of Poor or unsuccessful people. Look at the images hanging on the walls in your home, especially in your entrance, living room and your workspace. Are they representing poverty, depression or blockages? It's important that you do not hang images of people that are depressed, looking poor or begging at your entrance. Your entrance is the first impression of success and wealth when you or someone comes in to your home or workspace. Hang something more

inspiring, for example: Image of an award, a picture of victory, an eagle soaring, a positive phrase or happy people.

- Money energy requires oxygen at all times. Open your windows wide and often and replace recycled air with a fresh Qi. Place live plants, this purifies air and keeps the energy in your space vibrant and wealth-ready.

Clutter management

Letting go of the past is Forgiveness as is letting go of things that have negative connections or serve no worthwhile purpose. This makes space for positive replacements. Feng Shui recognises that clutter can make people feel disorganised, uncreative, tired, anxious and burdened Energy or Qi is all around us, all the time, the clutter is a clutter of energies.

Positive Qi can become blocked by clutter. When energy is blocked, it becomes stagnate and then turns to negative energy. That is why one of the main principles of Feng Shui is that you must de-clutter your home. It's important to remember that getting rid of the old makes way for the new.

Start by clearing out everything that doesn't need to be there. If you haven't used or thought about something in six months or more, unload it. In order to get new things in your life you have to release old things. Look around your home. Let go of Failure. If you have financial problems, let go of things, papers, files, pictures and items that are representing lack of financial abundance. Let go of anything representing your old business adventures, projects, jobs that didn't work out for you. Put them all in a box and store it somewhere to tell the universe there is space for a renewed success. Let go of everything, even old images, particularly of personal and work relationships that ended. Release it all.

When clutter is visible, your sub conscious mind sends a message of chaos to the universe. Keep your spaces orderly, everything must have its place, if it doesn't have a place, it is considered clutter. Keep walkways open and free for to Qi to flow.

Sometimes it can be challenging to get rid of things that we don't need, but in doing so, we free up more of our energy to devote to the things we want. If you resist letting go of items because you spent money on them, then consider selling them. You can hold a garage sale, list them on Craigslist or eBay. If you're worried you will need something as soon as you unload it, then you are holding on to old energy patterns that block your Qi moving forward and your resistance is indicating lack and limitation, a belief that you may not have enough to buy more or get it again. Even the thought of saving money by holding onto things for a later date is indicating lack and limitation, as well as inviting some adversity to occur.

Here's an example of relationships. When we hold on to the baggage from old relationships, they tend to carry over into new relationships, and this causes issues in the new relationship. If you were with someone for a period of time and they cheated on you, you may carry the belief that you have been burnt in this way, so you have built up resistance to complete trust and faith. This can spill over to your new partner and, even if they are not cheating, sometimes you feel there may be something they are not telling you. And it causes a fight until eventually you break up. It's the same concept with clutter in your home. If you carry all that old clutter around, there is no room in your life for new things to prosper. Abundance and prosperity will pass you by because you're too busy holding on to lack and clutter.

Your living areas

Represent the present. Too much clutter creates stagnant Qi as well as inconvenience and frustration. Remove items that are from previous ailments or items given to you that you do not particularly like. Place something that makes you feel good and makes you smile. Lilac represents the frequency of releasing, use lavender oils in your soaps, lotions and cleaning products to cleanse the stagnant, dense Qi.

Outside areas

Represents the present. Clear gardens of dried plants, or rubbish lying around, clean paths and maintain this, it allows the flow of positive Qi to enter. No faded, broken items or dried plants, the positive Qi is not present in these.

The Basement or under your home/office

Represents the past. This is better place to store things, however, too much stored indicates you are trapped in the past.

The attic

Represents the future. Too much stored here can block your future and the futures of generations to come. Avoid storage above the bedrooms or lounge room.

Improve your Qi flow with FORGIVENSS and RELEASE

-Clear and organise your home or workspace. To get the energy flowing, prepare your home or office by creating an open and uncluttered space in every room. Remove clutter, reorganise storage and clear obstructed spaces.

- Let go of possessions, emotions, and thoughts that keep you stuck.

- The colour violet represents forgiveness

- Elevate the level of Qi in your environment and yourself.

- Reliving old memories is stagnant Qi. Let go of the past, things that have no allocated space or serve no worthwhile purpose. And the things you have not used or thought about in six months or more, including clothing. Remember that getting rid of the old makes way for the new Qi. Move on to make new happy memories. Free up the stuck, dense energy to create a brilliant future

- Have a more positive outlook and focus on the things you are grateful for. Start a gratitude journal. Each day write three things you are grateful for.

- Clear and organise your home or workspace to get the energy flowing, and prepare for new people, experiences, and opportunities into your life. Create space for good fortune to enter your life by creating an uncluttered space in every room.

Activate Your Wealth Zones

A Feng Shui consultant uses the combination of Space Feng Shui and Time Feng Shui.

Space Feng Shui assessments determine the directions Qi flows in and around your physical environment. This includes General space orientation and activation of the home or office as well as activating and enhancing Personal Space Feng Shui based on an individual's Personal fortune directions to improve/increase Success, Health, Relationships and Growth. Time Feng Shui is the analysis of time cycles or Visiting Energy Assessments and the nature of specific energy flows of time cycles. All have their appointed compass direction, each of these nine directions have significant purposes, and the southeast corner of your home or workplace is your wealth sector.

Personal fortune directions or Personal Space Feng Shui as mentioned above can only be assessed on an individual basis where a person's birthdate and other factors are required for accurate assessment. General Space Feng Shui is universal, the following pages contain General Feng Shui for money and success to self-practice.

Activate your Home or Office For Success and Money

Feng Shui and quantum physics teaches that everything in our physical environment carries an energy that is moving our lives forward in that direction. By placing in our physical surroundings objects or images that have a positive personal meaning, we are activating and sending the Qi in this direction every time we look at it. Even if we think we do not see it any longer, it is still registering the message on a sub-conscious level.

Each of the eight compass directions, plus the center direction, is associated with a specific life area, element, number, shape, material, colour, and symbol. Some of the directions include a representative season and animal. Any area can be activated by placing specific elements, colours, items or images, in the specific compass direction and area of your home or workplace.

Compass directions for Success and Money for your home or workplace are north for clarity and self-empowerment. South for fame, recognition and celebration. East for focus and honesty. West for purity, transparency and joy. Northwest for transformation, supportive luck, business collaboration, magnificence and faith. Northeast for general and education collaboration. Southwest for compassion and Southeast for abundance, money, forgiveness and release.

Abundance

The Southeast represents material wealth, it is the prosperity sector for wealth, luxury and the extra things in life of every home, room and office. It also relates to personal abundance and opportunities in life as well as the direction of beneficial energy to strengthen your overall success and good fortune.

If you are struggling to make ends meet and want to gain financial abundance for your expenses, you want your completed projects to return the results you intended, you want to achieve greater results from your investment and effort; or to just attract increased income and opportunities. This is the direction to activate. Do the southeast direction of your home, yard and every work area.

However, before you activate your abundance in money you must appreciate money and what it can do for you. As mentioned in the introduction the lack of money or resources creates worry, stress and even conflict with our loved ones. This affects the positive flow of energy in many areas of life. Another aspect is how one feels about money, some have negative beliefs about it.

There are many conditioned beliefs in regard to money that were shared with us throughout time such as money is the root of all evil. This statement has been much distorted. Money is not evil, nor is the cup you drink from or the clothes you wear, they are all simply items. It is how one chooses to use money that can make an event or circumstance unpleasant or wonderful. Create a new energy you need to manifest your intentions. Abundance is everyone's birthright, not lack and stress. Have faith, love and know that each of us can and deserve all the comforts we choose. Fears or judgements are only influences from the environments we grew up in. Here is an excerpt from *Wallace Wattles, The Science of Getting Rich* to help you;

"There are three motives for which we live: We live for the body, we live for the mind, we live for the soul. No one of these is better or holier than the other; all are alike desirable, and no one of the three — body, mind, or soul — can live fully if either of the others is cut short of full life and expression."

"A person cannot live fully in body without good food, comfortable clothing, and warm shelter, and without freedom from excessive toil. Rest and recreation are also necessary to his physical life.

One cannot live fully in mind without books and time to study them, without opportunity for travel and observation, or without intellectual companionship. To live fully in mind a person must have intellectual recreations and must surround himself with all the objects of art and beauty he is capable of using and appreciating."

To live fully in soul, a person must have love, and love is denied fullest expression by poverty. A person's highest happiness is found in the bestowal of benefits on those he loves; love finds its most natural and spontaneous expression in giving. The individual who has nothing to give cannot fill his place as a spouse or parent, as a citizen, or as a human being. It is in the use of material things that a person finds full life for his body, develops his mind, and unfolds his soul. It is therefore of supreme importance to each individual to be rich."

"There is nothing wrong in wanting to get rich. The desire for riches is really the desire for a richer, fuller, and more abundant life — and that desire is praiseworthy."

To maximise your wealth, you can find the southeast corner of each room and place something that attracts wealth and create more cash flow. The best objects are those that use energy, such as fountains, fish tanks, or blossoming round leaves live plants. These items help keep the energy flowing through each room. Do not place dried flowers, the positive Qi no longer exists in these.

You can also place in the southeast corner of your lounge room or workspace an altar-like area where you hold the majority of your items that represent wealth. For example, this area is a great place to hang a vision board, pictures of things you want to buy, images or items that represent wealth to you, or framed money. Use gold frames, gold is the colour for abundance.

In order to attract, keep, as well as multiply the energy of abundance, there must be a good quality of energy in your space to allow the consistent flow of Qi. This is done by light, wind and decluttering.

Ensure the southeast is well-lit with natural or indoor lighting. Light as well as colour are our nutrients, particularly sunlight, this gives your environment and body enough nourishment. If the southeast in any spaces are limited with natural light, ensure that you use lamp. Dark areas and corners create dense, negative Qi.

Money energy requires oxygen at all times. We are fed by the air we breathe as well as our environment. Aerate your spaces to bring in new fresh Qi and replace recycled air. Ensure you maintain high levels of Qi by opening windows and doors wide and often, do whatever it takes to find solutions for better air in your home. Place live plants, this purifies air and keeps the energy in your space vibrant and wealth-ready.

As stated in the previous chapter clutter clearing is essential for creating a positive flow of Qi. All activations including colours, objects or plants will negate against the low, depressing energy of clutter. Unclutter your southeast direction, available space invites free flowing Qi. Clutter drains the energy. Open, clean, clear and organised space welcomes new opportunities and invites room for your abundance to improve, flourish and thrive.

Set your Intention. Clearly visualise your life with your ideal wealth and success goal. Write this in a journal. Write in the now as though you are watching a movie about it. The stronger and clearer you are in stating what you'd like, the easier it is for the universe to send you your heart's desire. Write a list of all the qualities wealth is to you and in the positive. Is it pay the bills, holidays, a beach house, more money with more free time, investments? What do you feel like? How would that look, feel, taste, smell? Bring that sense into your southeast with specific images, colours, and scents that reflect the energy you want. Do not place sad or dark images. Place images and items that represent wealth to send the message of abundance such as a money symbol, lucky bamboo, a Wealth Ship or something gold or gold in colour and place a wooden items. Ensure you place all images in a gold frame.

Water is an ancient symbol of abundance, it represents wealth and powerful to attract fresh Qi, place a small bubbling fountain in the southeast direction your home, lounge room or workplace. If you are unable to place a fountain use an image of water. Ensure the water is clear and moving. Do not put water features in bedrooms, kitchens or toilets. They will wash away your wealth. A water feature that keeps the water flowing represents a never-ending cycle in wealth. Place a Dragon beside the water feature to empower the water and bring you wealth luck. Do not place the Fire element in the north, fire evaporates water

Everything is Energy. Everything around you is energy including your wallet. This carries you more than you carry it! A wallet can help you attract and keep the ever-flowing energy of wealth. Your wallet is *the* home for your money. As with space Feng Shui the same basics apply to your wallet – clutter-free, order and beauty must be present for positive energy flow. No bursting seams or overflowing of old receipts, photos and cards that are rarely used. This speaks of poverty, scattered energy, fear and chaos. Ensure you wallet is clean, ordered and not damaged and place it in the southeast or north direction of your area of choice. Ensure it is the same and secure place each time and that can be easily reached. You should be able to find your wallet, immediately. Carry only what you need and have a clear system, show your money love and respect. Line it up so it is ordered and always leave space for more.

Crystals are a powerhouse for positive energy flow. They bring the essence of abundance from deep within the earth. Place a clear quartz crystal or pyrite in the southeast direction. Objects in purples, reds and greens also symbolise wealth and money. Purple amethysts and crystals are wonderful wealth Qi enhancers. Add purple accessories, colours and fabrics to the southeast. Purple includes plum, lavender, and lapis blues.

Ensure you keep your wealth from being cheated or robbed. The Chinese protection symbol against getting robbed is the rhinoceros or Chinese Fu Dogs. The rhinoceros should be brass or metallic with double horns. Place it outside your entrance, you can also wear this symbol for your own protection.

Activate your Home or Office For Success and Money

Your Personal Fortune Directions and Time Feng Shui for Money and Success

Your Personal Fortune directions are based on your Kua number, and has a greater effect for you personally than general space Feng Shui. The areas include success, relationships, health and growth, and is established by gender, as well as date of birth. Money is associated with success, and when you know your Personal Fortune Directions you can face it for added success, as well as place activations in these directions to amplify your personal success. There are four misfortune directions as well. When you are aware of these directions you can cure and ensure specific placements are not hindering your success. To establish the fortune colour, element, shape and fabric for you, your environment, your wallet and other aspects requires a Personal Fortune direction analysis. a Feng Shui Consultant is recommended.

There is also annual, monthly and 20 year cycle movements of energies called stars also known as Time Feng Shui. The Annual Wealth energy is called Star 8. The Wealth Star is based on your house or office building period and the direction. Each building contains within it a wealth area. For a precise analysis it is recommended to appoint a Feng shui Consultant.

Never place anything into your space that you do not love just because you are told you to do so. Feng Shui is about creating a positive flow of Qi as well as creating a living space that feeds your soul and uplifts your spirits. Objects you don't love will have the opposite effect. The more personal the objects are to you, the more Qi they will generate. Representations of items do not require to be only one thing such as Eastern symbols. An example is the Chinese symbolism for a tortoise, the Celestial Guardian of the North, this can be represented by any tortoise, live, image or object.

Power and Career

Feng Shui masters discovered through art, science and practice that certain parts of the environment corresponded to key areas in the lives of its occupants. They have shown through the centuries that improving your Luck is fast, easy, and within your control. By working with these energies, you can identify what is going on in an area of your life, and through Feng Shui practice enhance it by placing objects that would encourage the Qi to become activated.

In terms of career, money, and career growth. Your home or your workspace both must have positive vibration. This also includes you and your physical space. Your personal energy is connected to both your home and workplace and your career is directly connected to the North. The north direction represents future and your path from birth to death, your entire journey on this planet.

When you change the position of your desk or bed or change other things such as colours in your surroundings, the impact is immediate and direct. This also creates a positive spiral of energy upward that affects your life bringing luck and a positive flow. To improve your energy flow start by cleaning and organising your home or workspace, prepare your home or office by creating an open space in every room. Gather the clutter and place it in drawers and cabinets, or get rid of anything you do not require. Wipe the dust from your rooms and clean the floors. Remove dead as well as dried flowers, and place fresh bouquets if you like.

Activate your power position and path in life. North it is the general direction for creating your future when you choose to have more impact with your positive actions, feelings, and thoughts, feel safe and protected, and attract more praise for your talents and accomplishments. You may want to radiate more power and confidence or be in a more powerful position in your job. You have problems at work and want them to improve or you need pointers on your next career move is. Feng

Shui increases your power, especially when you feel it is diminished.

Ensure you sit on a strong, solid high-backed chair. Feng Shui requires that you feel the support of the universe in your life, your personal throne must support you in the back and a solid wall behind you provides better support than a door or window. Add a protection symbol represented by the tortoise. Place an object or image of a metal tortoise behind where you sit in your workspace. It is an energy enhancer for your career and will help attract a smooth grounding energy and stability for your business projects or promotions in your career. It also represents peace and longevity. You can also place a large plant, a small tree, or an image of a tree behind you to enhance the north direction.

Position your desk to see the incoming flow of people through the door. Do not sit directly in the flow from the door or have your back to the door. Seeing the incoming flow from where you sit ensures you can see the opportunities that come to you. You will make the right decisions because you can see all the angles and hear the right advisors. Also ensure you have at least three to ten feet of space between where you sit and the door.

The more space the longer the opportunity, this also applies to your bed.

Many opportunities come at night because dreams and inspiration influence great decisions. To remain in power as you sleep, position your bed so you can clearly see the door without twisting your body. Ensure your feet are not pointing directly at the door. Also ensure you have a solid wall and bedhead behind you for support.

Create your future by activating your desires. In the north direction of your lounge room, workspace and bedroom place artwork that has open views and high energy images, symbols of future projects or goals, new ideas you would like to explore, items connected to your present career or a new career you would like. Place images that best represent the essence of your career and display them as well as a bubbling fountain or an image of water. This will help generate more Qi to vitalise and improve the energy flowing to your career. The water must be moving, but not turbulent. Also place a jade Buddha is a symbol of good luck and fortune and is great for career and money. Do not put water in a bedroom.

In addition clean and organise your office, ensure you are surrounded with success reminders such as images of positive quotes, images of your own career highlights or photos of people you admire. Keep the air fresh and circulating, release the stale air by opening windows and doors. Also keep the space bright for positive flowing energy. Place lush green small plants. They will also keep your personal energy fresh and vibrant, which is a must if you want to attract lasting career success.

If you experience confusion as to which path to follow, or which step to take next in your career, place a map or globe of the world in the north direction. It opens up fresh energies on a subconscious level and helps you find your way.

Fame and Recognition
South is the general direction that represents success to the outside world for aspirations of fame, recognition, good reputation, promotions, upward mobility and acknowledgement of your achievement. This direction not only helps to inspire us internally but gets us noticed externally at the same time such as having more impact with your projects, being noticed for what you do, attracting more praise for your talents and

accomplishments, it helps you radiate more power and confidence or be in a more powerful position in your job.

The south sector belongs to the fire element which brings wisdom, clarity, brilliance, perception and intuition. It is important to note that if the north or southeast directions have been activated, the south must also be activated. If you create a product or service and wish to receive money as well as recognition for this you must be noticed by the outside world, therefore it is imperative that you activate south direction.

Place in the south direction of your home or workplace your ads, logos, marketing materials or a Laughing Buddha. For the fire element place the colour red and ensure the lighting is bright to enhance the Qi. Do not place blues and water symbols here as water puts out fire.

Energise the South direction with an item or image of its celestial guardian, the Phoenix. This represents opportunities that bring success and prosperity.

General Supportive Luck

Have more friends, enhance your general supportive luck and friendships, mentoring relationships, your relationship with your father, and relationships with your children by placing Items or images in the northwest of your Home, Office or Yard, such as Images of supportive kinds of relationships: fatherhood, personal pictures with your father, mentors, friendships, or an image of helping hands. Do not place Fire elements here. No wastebaskets, clutter, or yard waste in these corners because the accumulation creates density and slows the flow of positive Qi When you work in business with your friends, father, or children, enhance the Northwest area in your workplace as well.

The TRINITY of LUCK

In Feng Shui, there are three categories which describe the type of luck we experience in our lives, they are:

Heaven Luck- This refers to the karma, destiny, health types, astrological horoscope and the family environment you were born into and is determined by the cycles of time. This type of luck cannot be controlled. You can however, through astrological cycles or the Chinese Astrology Almanac, also known as the Tung Shu prepare for times when you are more likely to experience positive and negative points towards key areas in your life such as health, relationships, career, or finances. It helps to take note of astrological periods. This indicates where your key life lessons will be more likely to occur. Your astrological chart also helps determine areas where you are more likely to experience luck potential. These astrological events can affect communications, contractual problems, delays, travel, machinery breakdown and times of change and unexpected news. To make the most of your overall luck potential, you should develop a positive, progressive attitude while applying Feng Shui principles to your home and work environment, as well as keeping up to date with major astrological changes in your life. Luck is ultimately when skill and knowledge, plus the right attitude, meet opportunity. Feng Shui can help the flow of Qi that attracts positive energy, this increases your abundance opportunities.

Earth Luck - This type of luck is determined by our surroundings for example our home or workspace and the way in which we direct ourselves with positive or negative energy combinations, within and around the earth. This type of luck can be improved and enhanced when Feng Shui is correctly applied to your home or work environment. It deals with balance, element cycles, mathematical probability factors, magnetic orientation, surrounding landform and time dimensional analysis.

Human Luck - This refers to your personal attitude, education, managerial and financial ability, lifestyle, virtues, the choices that you make and your personal quest for knowledge. As an individual, you have full control over this type of luck, and when it is combined with Earth Luck through the correct application of Feng Shui, you increase your experience for greater harmony, contentment and success. To truly experience the joys which life can offer, you must first examine your attitude and sense of self. Change your attitude and you can quite literally change your life. You can utilise positive symbols, words and images within your surroundings to help focus and connect your personal aspirations with the appropriate Earth Luck location combinations.

- Learn to recognise your negative self talk. We all do it to some extent. Change it to an uplifting phrase.

- The positive and negative behaviours in your life have had many years to shape you into the unique individual that you have now become. Learn to look at yourself objectively in order to recognise certain conditioned responses and patterned behaviour, this can be enlightening.

- Acknowledge each positive step that you take forward.

- Surround yourself with positive friends and family who will encourage and support you.

- Actively seek to learn and experience as much as you can from the people and environment around you. Learn from someone who has what you want. Knowledge is life with wings. Find yourself a mentor someone who you aspire to be like and admire for what they have achieved in their life. Observe the ways in which they conduct themselves.

- If you find yourself feeling negative resolve it through forgiveness. You may not alter a situation immediately, but you can take full control of your response to the situation and how you ultimately deal with it.

General Collaboration

Improving collaboration amplifies your efforts. Remove any symbols that contradict collaboration such as: images of yourself alone; images of animals attacking, battles, or other tragedies, images of people or animals facing away from each other. Activating relationship directions of your workplace improves your professional collaboration. To increase collaboration, place the pictures or items for your activations together so they give a feeling of togetherness. Put these pictures in a fuchsia frame

-Learn from others, there are gems in all we experience

- Share the workload. This will invite a positive flow of Qi for all.

- Share a common sense of accomplishment. Be happy for another's success, when you rejoice for another your rewards increase.

Enhance Your Connection to Heaven

The direction connected to the Northwest is called Helpful People and Blessings or Connection to Heaven and help from Heaven, it also relates to patriarch and patronage luck representing the full force of Yang energy. This direction within the home or workspace aligns your connection with the outside world including your mentors, work colleagues, friends, networking, benefactors and business prospects.

Place an activation here for the energy to help attract beneficial people in your life. We all need somebody to help us. We all need a mentor. Mentors do not only refer to people who are in power who can teach us things or help us in achieving our goals, this also refers to people who may not be our senior in stature, age, experience, but are around us can is able to contribute to our success. Place silver bells and a singing bowl in this direction. Avoid water images as they will deplete the favourable energy.

In Feng Shui, by activating our Mentor's Luck we start to attract people who help us along the way. Begin by being positive yourself this starts the flow of a powerful positive aura, which in turn will attract people who are also positive.

This direction also supports the energy of travel, if you would like to travel more, express this energy here. Travel is also beneficial to health, new environments equals a new flow of Qi. Place travel photos, and maps. Photos of people who have helped you grow in life are also good to display or spiritual mentors, symbols, teachers, and angels that support us. Do not put a fire element, candles in the Northwest of home, lounge room, or other important rooms because it symbolizes fire at heaven's gate. If you have a fireplace in the Northwest, place a bowl of still water next to it, the water element represents diminishing the fire energy.

Business Collaboration

Enhance relationships with your business or work colleagues.

For better collaboration with your manager, supervisor, mentor, personal coach, or boss, activate the northwest direction in your workplace, it stands for hierarchy and is connected with heaven, the father, the stars, and the planets. Place a picture of you and your intended collaborator along with their business card attached to yours. If you want help from powerful and influential people, this is the sector to activate. Display a wealth ship (with sails, no cannon holes) here and pile up with coins, jewellery or gemstones.

For better collaboration with your work colleagues or business partners, activate the Southwest direction in your workplace. This direction represents general collaboration. Place a team picture or a ceramic circle of animals or people.

If you are in business with your romantic partner, mother, or children, also activate the Southwest in your workplace with personal pictures on display.

When working with others in your office, add a round table, this shape enhances collaboration and a mastermind of problem solving ideas.

Education Collaboration

For a student who would like to have a great collaboration with their teacher of knowledge and skills or mentor activate collaborative help with your studies or work. Place in your workplace or study books, study material or work related paper work in the northeast direction.

Areas in the environment

The art and science of Feng Shui is intricate and complex. Houses and their surroundings are studied carefully for their influence on people living in the house. Our environments are powerful energy attractors that may or may not be serving what it is we truly want to bring into our experience The quality of energy in your environment determines the quality of your wealth and success. When Feng Shui principles are implemented, this creates positive energy flow in the environment bringing more abundance and prosperity for all members, both young and old.

By incorporating Feng Shui principles, you can create a harmonious, prosperous space allowing the energy to flow in a positive manner. When your environment is relaxed and balanced, your mood will reflect this, and you in turn will become more relaxed and less stressed. Practice Feng shui in your workplace to create a space that encourages relaxation as well as productivity.

Lounge/Family room

Place a Bubbling fountain, a symbol of water, or an image of a bubbling fountain to activate items in the southeast area of your lounge room or workspace. Or a fish tank, fish are constantly in motion. As you feed the fish, imagine the Universe feeding you abundance.

Bringing life and energy to the southeast is important. The easiest way to do that is with live plants. Choose round leaves plants, they can even have flowers in red and purple to invite wealth into the room. Just remember that dead plants are a source of negative energy. If the plant is not blossoming, do not leave it sitting in your room to stagnate the flow you're trying to create. .

Dining Room

Hang a mirror with a gold frame reflecting the dining table. This doubles abundance. Place symbols of abundance in the dining area. You can add a gold bowl filled with diamond representations, gold objects and other symbols of abundance. A mirror also doubles the food on the table and diners, this promotes success in other areas such as health and relationships. Keep fresh fruit or flowers on the table. This brings life, energy. It also symbolises abundance as well as good health.

Bedroom

Most people spend one third of their lives in a bedroom, some such as teenagers can spend more. This area requires focus on creating good energy flow for your success.

Ensure you pay attention to your bed. If you feel particularly low in energy, it could be related to your bed. Something as easy as moving your bed can make you more money. Opportunities keep coming at night because dreams and inspiration influence great decisions. You will unexpectedly find yourself at the right place, at the right time, to meet the right people, to attract the highest energy, and live the richest life. To remain in power as you sleep position your bed in the command position where the headboard is against a solid wall and that you can clearly see the entry door. Avoid placing the bed in line with a doorway, this can cause feelings of vulnerability and defensiveness, depletes a room's energy, and it messes with your sleep patterns. The door should be visible from the bed. Also avoid alignment with the bathroom door, as this can contribute to feeling drained, tired or having restless sleep patterns. Ensure your bed is clean and tidy with fresh sheets, it's also important to clean the dust from your bed, dust is dense energy or negative Qi. Vacuum your bed once a week, and ensure you change the mattress every eight years, as recommended. This placement encourages the natural flow of Qi, which in turn promotes restfulness, sleep and motivation, all of which are conducive to a successful professional life.

To improve the wealth of your space, attach three coins tied together with a red ribbon on all four posts of the bed. Open your windows at least once a day to promote air flow and let fresh air into the room. Start your morning with natural light. Natural light releases positive energy, raises serotonin levels, and makes your workday more productive. Stale, stagnant air blocks energy. Hang three coins tied with a red ribbon by the window to keep the good energy in, or a six-rod hollow metal wind chime in the window. Wind chimes attract good chi and wisdom. Ensure that it is a six-rod hollow metal wind chime. This wind chime is the best moving metal activator because it removes the density of the earth by attracting the energy of the earth in its hollow tubes. Six rods are connected with wealth and 6 is the energetic number for metal. There are no substitutions for using these wind chimes.

Do not sleep under a window. Moonlight on the head, brings lack of focus during the daytime. Ensure your bed has balanced energy on both sides for example do not have one side of the bed up against a wall. Ensure both sides of the bed have a side table, light and a pleasant view. Position other furniture harmoniously. Good furniture arrangements play a significant role in Feng Shui. It is important clear the path to enter your bedroom, no matter what section of the house it's located in. Try to make sure that large furniture is not placed near the doorway.

Avoid storing a lot of electronics in bedrooms. The constant hum of electricity and blinking lights disrupts the flow of energy, and it is difficult to relax in that environment even when you are asleep. If you must have electronics in the room, be sure to put them away when you're not using them.

Ensure you do not have a mirror reflecting the bed. A mirror that reflects your image when you are in bed scatters thoughts and creates negative dreams. It's best to avoid putting a television in the room, this affects the energy in the room, and it also reflects the bed. If you choose to have this place a cover over it when not in use.

Ensure items in the room have a proper place. There must also be order to the room. Visual symmetry provides peace of mind, and it keeps the energy flowing through the room evenly.

Do not put water in the room, actual water or images with water. This attracts more unsettling dreams. No live plants or flowers because they have too much active yang energy for the bedroom, calm yin energy is required.

Avoid work related items or exercise equipment. The bedroom is a passive space, not yang energy. Place your work desk or computer elsewhere. If you have no other place for a home office ensure the computer and all the work related items are put away before going to bed so you do not see it from your bed. The also applies to exercise equipment, place it elsewhere, not under the bed otherwise the active energy will promote a restless sleep.

Exposed beams over a bed and a part of the body, creates problems in that area. When sleeping under a beam people have problems because these structures put pressure on their aura. Beams straight across over the head symbolises the guillotine and good energy will be cut off before it benefits you. Thin and sharp beams have greater impact than beams that are flat and wide. Diagonal beams indicate that the good energy will start to flow but will not finish right. Sitting under beams for several hours has the same effect as sleeping under beams. Move your bed if is under a beam. If your space is limited and your bed cannot be moved, cover the beam with fabric or paint the beam to match the ceiling. No see through fabric.

Sleeping in a room where the street traffic faces you directly is a negative Feng Shui situation. The lights of the cars represent the eyes of the tiger stalking and attacking you, this creates stress. Place window coverings such as heavy curtains to block out the lights and hang a pakua mirror on the outside of the window. These are special 8-sided mirrors used to cure negative Qi.

Allow natural light in during the day, good air flow, do not store anything under the bed, and keep your wardrobes clean and organised.

Ensure you have a solid headboard this represents support, and energetically brings both sides of the bed together, creating harmonious union. If possible, avoid metal bedframes they enhance the water element and water should never be in the bedroom, metal is yang Qi and attracts unsettling dreams.

Too much stuff piled in a bedroom (or any room for that matter) is a huge energetic distraction that subconsciously pulls us away from our focus. The bedroom should be a space designed for rest, rejuvenation, and relief from the outside world. Remove the clutter such as computers, exercise equipment, paperwork, kids' projects, or piled clothes, find a place for them. Just be careful not to clutter up another part of your home, everything must have its place or it is considered as clutter.

Make your bed, every morning it shapes the day for success, transforming chaos into order. And since we spend a third of our lives in bed, this enhances devotion to yourself.

Your bedroom, bathroom and kitchen are your home trinity, ensure they are clean and uncluttered with no expired products. This will reflect in the energy of success if it one or more are left unattended.

- Sleep in a power position so you can clearly see the door and you have a solid wall behind you.
- Do not put water in the room, actual water or images with water.
- No live plants or flowers.
- No mirrors reflecting the bed.
- Have a solid headboard

Bathroom and Kitchen Areas

Clutter management in the bathroom and kitchen is required as in all other areas in your environment. Ensure your kitchen stove and refrigerator are clean, has no expired products, is orderly, and also in good working order. Do not let dirty dishes pile up or hang a towel through the oven handle. The stove is identified with wealth, it is a fire element of the home. The fire element is associated to the south and brings in fortune. To improve the flow of wealth in your life, ensure your stove is not stacked with pots and pans.

Fire placement in our environment affects our physical self and our homes health and longevity. If a stove or fireplace is incorrectly placed it can bring sickness, financial problems and misfortune. When fire is correctly placed it can support the health, prosperity and status of your family and also increase the value of your property. Kitchens are vital to a home's overall health. The placement of your appliances is more important than the actual direction your kitchen faces, because incorrect appliance placement can create negative Qi. A fire placement analysis of your kitchen is advisable. This assessment includes Personal fortune directions or Personal Space Feng Shui and can only be assessed on an individual basis where a person's birthdate and other factors are required for accurate assessment.

The Personal success direction of the main breadwinner is considered and important with appliance placement. If the stove and sink are directly opposite or in line with each other, hang a pakua crystal between them. However, it is recommended that you appoint a Feng Shui Consultant for exact analysis.

For General Space Feng Shui;

It's very important that the doors in the kitchen do not lead directly into the front or back doors. This kind of alignment means the Qi energy rushes through the kitchen and out of the house. This creates unbalanced Qi that brings misfortunes to those in the home. Place a mirror at the entrance of the kitchen to cure it.

Water dripping from your faucets or pipes will deplete your finances. Fix broken or leaking taps, pipes or toilet. Maintenance and care of these helps keep the good energy in the house, which then invites abundance.

Drains in sinks of the bathroom or kitchen can wash away money Qi. Plugging sinks with rubber stoppers when they are not in use to prevent the energy from flowing down the drain is good practice. You can also use rocks or pebbles instead of a rubber stopper. The rocks help form a barricade and create a pleasing visual display.

Keep brooms and mops stored in closets. These items are used to clean up dense negative Qi.

Ensure that your bathroom is clean, and organised and has a sense of beauty and pampering energy. Do not place photographs of friends or family members, as well as awards. These are drain areas, this tells the Universe you are flushing it all away. Also ensure the toilet lid is down and bathroom door closed.

Front Door
Your entry point is also known as the mouth of Qi, and this includes your front door. It is the energy connection of your home. It is where the Qi enters along with what you and others bring or take with you. When you leave, you take what you're feeling with you into your day. When you come home, you bring in all that has happened to you throughout the day. The first priority for your mouth of Qi is to clear the clutter from around your door. If you and your family store shoes, coats, equipment, toys, or any other items by the front door, move them. The clutter blocks the free flow of energy and prevents it from entering your life.

In Feng shui, the view you first see as you open your front door is very important, as is the view from your bed. They set the energy you and your body is receiving throughout the day. Ensure your eyes have views that make you feel good.

Corners are famous for retaining energy this can be either stagnant or vibrant, all depending on your efforts. A strong corner will actively draw in the incoming Qi. The corner that is closest to the main door and diagonally from it will absorb and retain a big portion of Qi, ensure these areas are clean, clutter free and place your activations to express the energy and welcoming abundance.

Surround yourself with symbols of abundance and place a sailing ship, also known as a wealth ship coming into your home. Make it as large as possible. Place in the ship symbols of wealth such as coins, gemstones, gold or gold representations. Ensure the ship is not sailing out of your home and that it has no cannons. Display it near your entrance on a low bench or table.

Place a three legged toad under a table, bench, sofa or chair diagonal to the front entrance. The money toad assists if you are troubled with bills or overspending. A three legged bull frog or toad holding coins in its mouth is very fortunate in terms of wealth. It is the guardian of house wealth.

Workspace/Office

The workplace is one of the key areas in which Feng shui should be implemented if you wish to manifest your intentions, clear your mind, promote better focus, and produce high quality work that your clients, bosses, and co-workers will admire.

Whether you work in a cubicle, at home, or in a spacious corner office, you can employ the tools used in Feng shui to bring more prosperity into your life, creativity and passion into your work, as well as more calmness into your space.

Keeping the office neat and tidy is very good because energy can flow freely. Do not gather unnecessary things in your office. The entrance to your office is a key component because it is what allows energy to flow freely into and out of your space. Ensure it is free of clutter. Also, the door to your office should open completely without anything getting in the way this indicates you will have your physical door wide open to welcome new clients, new work, and more money.

Place a dragon or horse to increase your success chances. The dragon is very powerful and fortunate in traditional Feng shui. The dragon claw is a symbol of wealth, power and a source of opportunities. The golden dragon can be placed in East for wealth and abundance. The horse carries the energy of success, fame, freedom and speed. Place it in north, this enhances your career.

Wind chimes attract good chi. Hang a wind chime over your desk or work space to increase positive Qi flow. Ensure that it is a six-rod hollow metal wind chime. This wind chime is the best moving metal activator because it removes the density of the negative Qi in its hollow tubes. Six is the energetic number for metal. There are no substitutions for using these wind chimes. For example, bells do not work. You can also hang wind chimes in windows that you open frequently to invite abundance into your home or workspace.

Display your products or services at the entrance to the workplace, even if people do not come there. Hang letters of recognition, awards, and pictures of the famous people. Place products on red fabric and surround them with golden coins. Red represents fire and fame, and gold represents metal and money.

The colours for your walls will ultimately depend upon the line of work that you are in. For example, if you work in a medical office, an environment in which you will be greeting anxious clients, calming colours, such as blue or green, on the walls should be used. To build positive relationships with clients in a professional business setting, use earth tones, such as terra cotta. Hang motivational artwork that encourages team collaborations on the northwest and west directions of your office space. To generate more wealth, place plants in the southeast and east directions, such as bamboo. Also place a small water fountain in the north direction that focuses on the energy of moving water. This will energise your career.

Arrange the surface of your desk with Feng Shui principles. The nine directions or bagua is a map that can be applied to your desktop as well as your computer, just as it would be applied to the floor plan of a home or office. Different areas of the bagua are associated with different areas of your life, for success and wealth, place as follows:

- The front left corner of the desk is associated with wisdom. Place the colour blue here, as well as symbols of things you would like to learn, can help you acquire more knowledge and that can help you in your career.

- The center front of the desk represents your career and should be clutter free. The dominant colour here is black, place some motivational quotes here.

- The front right corner represents helpers and travel. Place the colour grey here, as well as contact information, such as an address book, your phone, or a travel guide or photo of a vacation spot.

- The right side center of the desk represents your creativity and focus. To boost this place the colours silver, gold, white, and copper also add inspirational materials, such as quotes or books.

- The center back of your desk represents fame, recognition and your reputation. Place the colour red here and a nameplate, your business cards, or an image of yourself accomplishing something great.

- The back left corner of your desk represents wealth. Place the colour purple here. This is the area to focus on if you wish to attract more money. Place a plant with round leaves or any valuable object here. It is also an ideal spot for a computer. For the computer place icons such as your email, internet browser, or photo folders in the southwest of the screen which is the top right hand corner of the computer screen to enhance your general relationship and collaboration flow. At the bottom in the middle place your most important files and financial programs. At the bottom left corner place your agenda, and important personal papers. For Personal fortune directions, this can be established through a Personal Feng Shui analysis by a Feng Shui consultant.

Activate your Home or Office For Success and Money

For those who have a home office or work from home, you can apply the same Feng Shui principles as in any other work environment. Keep the entrance of your home neat, clean, and free of clutter, including the entrance to your office space. Even if clients do not attend this workplace this is essential in opening the flow of energy and welcoming positive improvements to your work life. The ideal area for a home office is close to the front of the property and to the front door. This is the area where a lot of energy can flow in to inspire you. Place your desk in the farthest corner so that you have a view of the entire room and the entrance. Do not have your back toward the door.

Your office should have yang energy. Home offices in the bedroom bring too much active energy into what should be a very passive room. If there is no other place to have a home office, ensure you put the computer and all the work related material away before going to bed so you don't see it from your bed.

Place all five elements in your workspace for balance; use water to inspire communication, metal to encourage prosperity, earth to promote long-standing relationships and balance in the workplace, fire to boost productivity, and wood to allow your creativity to flow.

Outside Areas

Outside areas follow the same principals as the inside environment. The wealth sector is located in the southeast corner of the yard. Ensure that the yard is properly trimmed and cleared of rubbish. Plant a garden and install a fountain or a fish pond. You can also include other symbols of wealth, such as a windmill, wind chimes, or weather vanes. Place red and purple flowers in the area, and the lawn furniture in groups of four, six or eight. You can use many of the same activations you used for the wealth sectors inside your home.

Do not renovate your home and then dig a pond if you are living inside the house. The digging of a trench represents loss in your money and wealth. Build a pond up without digging the ground.

Cleansing

Energy can neither be created nor destroyed; rather, it transforms from one form to another. When unpleasant feelings linger, space cleansing the environment transforms the energy to positive Qi leaving it lighter, healthier and happier, this creates more success. Everything that happens in an environment including conflict, trauma, and illness leave imprints and can attract other unwanted dense energy unless they are intentionally cleared. Subtle traces of past events can make places feel happy or sad. Replacing old carpet or furnishings, clutter management and redecorating all help to transform the negative dense Qi as well as cleaning the environment with lavender oils. Place a few drops of lavender oil in your cleaning products.

Express Happiness

Quantum physics states like attracts like energy. An environment that is clean, clutter free and loved will attract and promote harmony and happiness. Organise your spaces so that everything has its place. Most importantly, express love and care with all your home and workspace contents, this indicates good support, care, happiness and well-being.

General

.

There can be many subtle factors in an environment that supports us with either positive or negative results. Awareness and observation can move you from the negative to the positive flow.

Keep things clean, in working order and organised.

Place live round leafed plants throughout to encourage the growth of wealth, with the exception of the bedrooms, do not place water images or live plants in the bedroom, this indicates drowning in adversity while you sleep. Bamboo plants are seen as fortunate in the Chinese culture, also anything with round leaves as the shape of the leaves resemble coins.

Place your images in gold looking frames. The more gold you surround yourself with, the more gold will come towards you.
Walk around your home or workspace. Are you stopped by furniture or do you stumble on a rug? Do you have a hard time opening doors? Air should flow around everything in your home. Move furniture away from walls, even if just a couple of inches. Pull furniture pieces together to create an area where air can flow around. Use your windows. Natural light is very important and brings with it positive energy.

Windows should never be blocked. In the practice of Feng Shui, mirrors are used to reflect energy into other areas of the home, ensure mirrors are not reflecting doors, it will bounce the energy back out. Mirrors require proper placement, they can dramatically shift the flow of energy in any given space. Mirrors also bring a sense of refreshment and calm. Direct the flow of Qi with mirrors, lights, plants, colours, and items. Some obstacles are good, because they slow rushing Qi and enhance Feng Shui, however, some are bad, because they collect and spread stagnant Qi. Sense whether the obstacles feel good or bad. To direct the flow of energy down a hall to rooms such as the sleeping areas or workspace, hang a mirror or an image with reflective glass opposite the door to each room. When an obstacle blocks the flow of Qi, such as a plant, place a mirror so that it can reflect the energy toward thee direction you want the Qi to flow.

Add indoor plants and trees whenever you want growth. Avoid the cactus, as spikes invite criticism when grown inside. The Qi or life-force of the plant will energise the space as well as naturally remove indoor toxins and purify the air we breathe. Just remember that dead plants are a source of negative energy. If the plant is not blossoming, do not leave it sitting in your room to stagnate the flow you're trying to create. If you want to be more productive at work, plants on your desk or home office bring positive, creative energy to your work environment.

Add some motion to a space that is stuck. A stuck space usually reflects a stuck life. Move things around the room this helps liven the atmosphere. The Feng shui number to help guide you through this process of getting unstuck is twenty-seven. Just by moving twenty-seven things around a space whether it's a paper clip or a desk can bring positive energy to a room that was previously lacking it.

The west is the area of purity and communication. Enhance this direction in your lounge/family room or workspace with items or pictures related to children such as children playing. You can also place an item or image of a laughing Buddha to increase happiness. If work with children, also activate the West direction in your workplace with pictures of the children you work with or care for.

Along with structure, items and colours your words create your environment, too. Something as subtle and innocent as a word enters our subconscious and affects how we feel. Be conscious on your vocabulary, and watch it shape your path. When we honour ourselves with good words, including praise for ourselves and others, we fuel our ability to live a good life.

Many have discovered the benefits of Feng Shui. If you would like to invite more wealth and abundance in your life, begin with these principles and expand the energy in your home or workspace. In the eastern culture, those who find success through Feng Shui practises do not sell their homes once they become millionaires. They keep it for luck and continued good energy, even if they move into a new house.

Everything we do is controlled by the energy we put into it. Feng Shui helps release stagnated energy and escorts in good energy. Those who find the right balance in their homes discover that when the right energy is in place their wealth increases much more than just getting by and paying the bills. Feng Shui is an ancient science and art that many people have had success with, and it's possible for you to have that same success, as well

For complete and comprehensive balancing, activations and cures for your home or workspace, contact a Feng Shui Consultant. Please note: Direction identification with a compass is the only way to get an accurate reading of your environment. More than half of the people who conduct their own Feng Shui compass readings do it incorrectly. It's imperative that it's accurate; creating analyses based on inaccurate readings is worse than doing nothing to correct or remedy inauspicious elements in your home.

Wealth enhancers

Feng Shui cures obstacles strengthens intentions and addresses how the Qi flows through an environment. A value of Feng Shui is to bring our awareness to those areas of our life which are not in harmony with our intention. There are several approaches to making these adjustments and enhancements by adjusting the home or workplace environment, even ourselves. We can remove negative Qi and other dense factors that distract, slow down or, in some other way, divert our intention for desired success.

The Bagua directions of a home or workplace divides the structure or individual spaces into nine areas of life activity and these are connected by distinct energy fields of the spaces along with objects, images, plants animals and people. Through people and animals emotions and personal practises are also emitted. When you improve the energy of your home, you change yourself and your life and by applying the Feng Shui principles for self enhancement you evolve to fulfil your desires. Author *Napoleon Hill* explains, *"Our brains become magnetised with the dominating thoughts which we hold in our minds, and, by means with which no man is familiar, these 'magnets' attract to us the forces, the people, the circumstances of life which harmonise with the nature of our dominating thoughts."*

CLARITY

Clarity is the quality of being easily understood, expressed, remembered and of being easily seen or heard

Feng Shui principles assist you in communicating more clearly by expressing your needs and desires openly, earnestly and wholly. Through establishing and applying your desires in your environment it creates impressive results from your efforts and avoids misunderstandings.

Clarity begins with deciding what you want. What kind of a success. How do you see a harmonious collaboration? Prioritise areas where you require fast results. Determine exactly what you want to accomplish. Bring a clear, accurate message of your desired outcome for your wealth and success. Place symbols, images or objects reflecting the outcome that you want to create. Let go of images that no longer clearly represent your intentions. Take care of what has not been completed now, just by starting and ticking off even your simplest tasks invites the positive Qi of clarity.

To send the best message about abundance and invite clarity, clean water features. Light up your home, workplace, yard and entry. Add bright objects and plants. Place happy items an image in the eight directions including the Centre of your home or workspace that represent vitality, freshness and joy.

Ensure the entrance to your home or workplace has clear messages showing the world to recognise and respond to your personality or business as well as indicating that a very successful person is inside. Also Place happy items or images outside. Do not hang dark or depressing images.

CELEBRATION

South stands for fame and recognition as well as music, celebration, and festivity, activate the South area by placing orange objects in lounge room or workplace. Unless you want to get pregnant do not activate celebration in the bedroom.

Celebrate your efforts and accomplishments, changes, significant dates and celebrate yourself! Cooked a great meal, celebrate, completed your tasks, celebrate, cleaned your workspace, celebrate. Add the positive flow of celebration to anything you choose to rejoice for.

Manifest more joy showing off your awards and place them in gold frames to invite abundance. This will give you more to celebrate.

Celebrate your accomplishments by throwing a party. Do not wait for others. Create celebrations for yourself. Feng Shui is a consistent celebration of positive flowing Qi. Include children in your parties, because they represent the fortune of the family.

HONESTY and HONOUR
Honour is connected to the east and power of the dragon, a symbol of power, truth, and magic. Place Dragon Symbol or object in your workspace or lounge room lower than eye level so it does not overpower you and enjoy the Dragon's precious cosmic breath.

Improve Human Luck: Feng Shui helps create an environment to change old habits, create more self-discipline and double your talents to their full potential. HONOUR is important, Eastern cultures practice Honour.

When the flow of life is good, ride the wave. When the flow of life is not great, check to see if it is keeping you from doing what you want to do. Contemplate your behaviour. Are your actions, thoughts and feelings honourable? If not what mental programs can you change, and emotions can you release.

Keep structure and good life management, practice self-help/development. These are a strong indicator of how we can change our programs. Discipline yourself to fulfil your destiny and to fully express who you are. Make it easier to stick to your intentions and actions with your family and clients. Surround yourself with people who are truthful. Be more honest with yourself and others.

Improve Heavenly Luck: Practise spiritual lessons, Qigong, yoga, prayer, meditation and positive affirmations.

Improve Earth Luck: Your environment, home and workplace, is a greater body surrounding your physical body. Every object in your home or workplace is like a cell in the greater body. And as part of the unified field of the whole, will affect your body and physical experience. There are unseen links of energy between every material thing. All part of the Quantum Physics field. This can be improved with Feng Shui practices by allowing the positive flow of Qi.

For your workspace display a pair of Fu Dogs at the entrance door to protect you against office politics and corporate power struggles.

PURITY

There are 5 levels of purity: Physical Home, office and body, Etheric, Emotional, Mental and Spiritual

Creating purity is essential if your thoughts and feelings are cluttered or chaotic, you are addicted to something or you feel abused or that people violate your boundaries.

Meditations, or exercises such as Qigong and yoga assist in creating stillness within the active mind. Visualise the light of the sun in your body and home with a light meditation. Open the windows and doors to bring in light and activate your senses. When natural light is low, use lamps in the dark areas. Ensure the four corners of each room in your home or workspace are well-lit. If you are unable to light all four corners of each space, ensure that every corner of your lounge room or workspace has light.

Clean your home or workspace with lavender oils mixed in with your cleaning products. Wash your physical body every day.

Use lavender soaps or add lavender oil to your shower gel, lavender helps release toxins and old energies from your aura. Breathe air charged with negative ions, consider using an ioniser air purification system.

To invite purity into your body and new possibilities into your life, create space for what you want. Even the best activations are impeded upon in a cluttered or dirty environment, ensure you dust your furniture too.

Do not display broken objects. The life force or Qi in these objects are broken and gluing does not restore the Qi.

JOY
The West is the direction for Joy it also represents communication, and children's luck.

If you would like to appreciate everything your senses experience or you lack joy, feel sad or are depressed. Place fun, humorous items here. Add fabrics, colourful artwork, bright pillows or objects bright colours to lead eyes from colour to colour. Peach and orange are the best for joy, red and warm yellows add joy too. Activate in the lounge room for everyone to invite more joyful communication. Place joyful images, toys and smiling people. Allow more sunlight to enter the spaces and open windows to let the wind bring new Qi into the home. If you cannot open your windows, use air fresheners and burn candles. White and black colours do not create joy. Exposed beams in your entrance or lounge room can create sadness for everyone in the family, cover them in fabric or paint them the same colour as the ceiling.

TRANSPARENCY

Invite clearness of mind, body, emotions and environment. Become more organised and get your business or personal records in order

Physical transparency:

In any room or area, donate, sell, or remove everything you do not need or do not love.

Entryway: When you come home, make sure your first view is clean and uplifting. The entrance to the home is the start of the flow of Qi, so always clean the entryway even if you cannot clean the rest of the home. Do not place coats and shoes within view in the entrance. Put them away in closets or in a shoe box. Keep your rubbish bins out of sight from the entrance.

Bedroom: Make beds every morning. Hang clothes in closets.

Lounge Room and workspace: Ensure these spaces are clean and uncluttered. Clean the windows and the window coverings regularly. Vacuum pet hair from furniture and carpeting. Do not leave books, magazines, or remote controls lying around. Before going to bed, tidy up to create a fresh start for the next day.

Kitchen: Discard old food, expired products, old spices or baking ingredients. Carefully wash all kitchen surfaces. Use cleaning products with lavender essential oil. Reorganise everything that is left, from food in the fridge to the items in cupboards and drawers and on countertops.

Laundry: Ensure the room is always closed off and dirty laundry is in laundry baskets.

Dining Room: Always clean up immediately after meals and place fresh flowers or a bowl of fruit on the dining table.

Landscape: Place flowers close to the entrance. No old cars, bikes, or general rubbish lying around. Keep ornaments and garden features fresh and clean. Paint or stain the fence. Keep garden furniture and umbrella fresh and not faded. Remove sick or dead plants and trees. The positive Qi has gone from these.

General: Ensure that people can easily find the entrance and turn the light on when it is dark. Every year, place a new door mat. This mat should be solid, no holes and should not have company logos or anything that can represent you, such as your family name. This indicates others overpowering you.

Etheric transparency

The etheric field is the energy body known as the first layer in the human energy field or commonly known as the aura. This field has less dense Qi than the Qi that surrounds the physical body. This energetic body or aura is fed by the air we breathe and the impact of our surroundings. Our etheric field is influenced by the level of Qi in a room. Low energy levels of Qi create negative thoughts and depressed feelings where high energy levels of Qi help us feel raised and happy. Ensure you maintain high levels of Qi by opening windows and doors. An oil burner, incense, ioniser or air purifier will enhance the positive flow. Ensure the air you breathe is clean. Be mindful of the images, objects, and paintings you display, this can create a negative impression on you.

Emotional transparency

Emotional fields from you and your family or past inhabitants may linger in your home or workplace. There may have been a break up or constant fighting. Place a little salt and rice in all of the corners of your spaces as a gesture of abundance and gratitude and remove it after one day. Also place water with sea salt in the centre of the home or workspace for seven days.

If you are experiencing arguments this may be associated with your kitchen. If your stove is opposite a sink this indicates disharmony, fire fights with water, water boils. Hang a pakua crystal between the stove and sink to unify fire and water. Door handles can also be associated with arguments if they hit against each other. Tie a red ribbon to the handles to symbolically establish unity between these arguing door handles then cut the ribbon evenly and tie them onto the handles.

Mental transparency:

Occasional sanctuary is required in our lives, particularly when you want to put ideas into action, slow down, restore clarity or when you want to be more relaxed mentally. For mental transparency create a room with less furniture, fewer books, fewer ornaments, and fewer things to tend. It can also be a chair and window focused on a view that is spacious or a bathtub filled with essential oils and natural suds. These are vital spaces to recharge our own energetic batteries, after all we are beings that contain electricity.

Also clean your desk when you finish working to be ready for fresh ideas.

FAITH

In Feng shui wealth means having more business, assets and properties that put money in your pocket and grow like a tree.

Activate your Home or Office For Success and Money

Your assets will multiply when you harbour feeling of abundance and wealth.

You must have faith, remind yourself to say this, either to yourself or aloud "No matter what, I always have plenty and some to spare." You simply need to get out of your own way, remove fear or doubt to attract the wealth you choose.

Also if you are dubious about spending money, you keep it for a rainy or in the bank. Then you send a message to the universe "I don't have enough money". So the universe will create scarcity. The more money you give the more money you will have. Money is energy release that energy and you will attract like energy, only in greater quantities. Donate some money to charity, help somebody, buy presents for people or buy something you like. All this creates feeling of abundance.

Have a strong belief and trust in yourself as well as with the ancient art of Feng Shui. Create the new energy you need to manifest your intentions. Change the way you think, feel, and act. Apply the principles and invite your chosen positive destiny to unfold. Have patience with yourself and others. Recognise the results from your Feng Shui practices. Positive and negative responses can occur as you begin making changes. Respond in a positive way, and feel relief that there is finally a logical explanation for misfortunes in your life. Feng Shui changes can stir up energy and temporarily upset order, but it will calm down as the energy finds a new order. If you resist you lose focus and concentration. Resistance leads to fear and anger, have faith in your choices.

TRANSFORMATION

Have you ever thought, if only! Or if I could turn back time. **Forgive and release the past,** say goodbye to old behaviours and beliefs that no longer serve you, and say hello to a more positive incarnation of yourself, there always has and always will be time, life offers to many wonderful opportunities, you just have to invite them in and **lay the groundwork for a better tomorrow to welcome your new success for what you truly desire.**

Boost your triumphs, live a more conscious lifestyle, get the support you need to pursue your dreams. Change the way you feel in your surroundings, change your thought patterns or how you feel about yourself and recognise your transformations.

By applying these Feng Shui practices you have placed yourself in a transformation whirlwind, a waterfall of change. Some people feel overwhelmed and disoriented, which indicates that something is changing. Things must change to allow for the new to come. *Einstein's definition of insanity, "Insanity is doing the same thing over and over again and expecting different results.".* You are sane! Stay with it and look for the positive changes from your new energy flow!

Ask yourself, do I feel:
Happy and more confident that everything will be all right. Peaceful in my own home or workspace. Excited about my life and the changes I want to create. Comfortable in my space and no longer running away from it. A need to change many things in my life. A sense of accomplishment because I have made more changes in one week than I have in years. Able to handle things and climb out of a depression. Open to others and myself.

How has my thinking changed? Do I feel less fear, doubt, limitation, or loneliness? Do I express more power, self-esteem, and success?

Notice the changes in your **career.** You may receive an award, more compliments for your work, or more benefits as compensation for your work. You may change careers or suddenly get promoted or fired but be happy in either event because it is perfect for you.

Notice the changes in **your finances.** Maybe your stocks go up or your investments that have never paid off start bringing in money. Perhaps your cash flow improves, or you get an unexpected return on your taxes. Maybe you are able to sell your place for a great profit, or you receive an unexpected bonus from work. You might start donating to a good cause.

Notice other changes such as your activity level. You might complete little jobs around the house, spend more time playing with your children or associating with friends, take up painting or writing, or express your feelings better. People around you may be offering more encouragement to pursue your dreams, or help you find the right resources.

Start a positive flow journal. Observe and record positive changes in your life. Write gratitude statements. Write in your journal daily, use blue ink, this is the colour for power. Recording your positive flow will enhance a chain of positive change in your own experiences and empower others to become active in their own good fortune and luck.

FOCUS

When focus is in balance you have fewer distractions and stronger concentration, stay focused on your goals, it improves your motivation for finishing projects you start and helps to recover from conditions or circumstances that diminish your focus.

To maintain focus decluttering all your spaces in the home, workplace and yard is imperative. Everything must have its place and there must be order. Even when items are in a cupboard or drawers, it must be easily accessible and not jammed full of things that fall out or must be removed to get to other layers.

In business, always declutter your desk and workplace before end the day. Return everything to its best Feng Shui position.

A variety of influences such as architecture, furniture, plumbing, colours, shapes, objects, symbols, landscape, and surrounding environment can lead to an inability to focus. Below are features and factors in your home or workplace that can interfere with focus, and what can be done to activate greater focus right away.

Poison Arrows
Any architectural features, furniture and pointed objects that aim toward you are considered poison arrows. For example,

corners of tables, desks or any corner of two walls that are in line with where you work or sleep.

A poison arrow directed at your body as you work will interrupt your focus. If you notice poison arrows where you sit or sleep from cabinets or bookcases place fabric or an item to cover the arrow. Ensure that all books on shelves, even shelves with doors, are flush with the edge of the shelf. This prevents shelves from creating a horizontal cutting energy that disturbs focus.

COMPASSION

Create a gentle ease of love and support in the way you relate to yourself and others. *"Be gentle first with yourself if you wish to be gentle with others." ~Lama Yeshe.*

When we feel compassion for others, we feel kindness toward them, empathy, and a desire to help. It's the same when you are compassionate toward yourself. Self-compassion creates a caring space within you that is free of judgment. An important part of living a happy and fulfilling life includes being part of sharing, helping and supporting people you care about. It also includes being kind to strangers, and learning to replace envy and anger with understanding and empathy. Allow yourself to see that *everything* around you is sacred.

Enhance compassion in the southwest direction of your lounge room or bedroom by placing an image or statue of your 'Mother of Compassion': Kuan Yin, Mother Mary, Tara, Mother Theresa, Isis or someone who represents compassion to you.
-Feel more compassion for yourself, others, and for the world you live in
- Go easy on yourself when you try new things or make mistakes
- Show trust in others and treat them with patience and gentleness
- Have patience to listen to your inner voice and the advice of others
- Be more open to others

EMPOWERMENT/SELF-EMPOWERMENT

Manifest Your Power by being open to transform your life. When you start to change things, make the changes with the right attitude. Proceed fearlessly. Do not complain about the changes you need to make, or it will block the ease of making them. Look for support available to you and believe you will have all the help you need. Let go of things and situations with joy. When something does not serve you anymore, be thankful for what you received from it. Recycle it to bless someone else. Place ornaments and move furniture with a sense of blessing. In between every change, take time to experience the impact and enjoy the process.

--Forgive yourself and release the past. Write a list of what you forgive yourself for or say it out aloud.

-Have courage to make necessary changes

-Create collaboration with all of the support available to you

-Love yourself and release judgment.

- Be more outgoing

- Learn how and when to say no. This is a crucial step towards reclaiming your personal sense of empowerment. You control your own choices.

MAGNIFICENCE

Create splendour in your surroundings. Believe in the greatness of your talents and accomplishments. Feel radiant, appreciated and enthusiastic. Enjoy recognition of your reputation and accomplishments

To double the positive effects of all activations, activate magnificence. Remove the clutter. Dust your spaces, dust is density, it keeps the wind and water from flowing. Metal objects must be shiny and radiant.

Add magnificence to your entryway, which is the first view of your home or workplace. Remove dust and all clutter from the entryway or entrance hall including delivered mail and boxes. Keep shoes, coats, and accessories hidden in a closet or wardrobe. Add an image of your products, services, and company logo. Double the size of a small entry with a mirror and use the mirror to guide Qi toward the main area. Also hang a crystal chandelier in your entrance or your dining room.

In your dining room place crystals and metal objects that are polished and radiant. Light candles in silver candleholders. Hang a mirror with a gold or silver frame to reflect the dining table to double your magnificence and abundance. If you have a wooden table, polish it to give the appearance and feeling of being alive otherwise, it has no Qi.

Place fresh flowers in strategic places such as the entrance, as a symbol of welcome, on the dining table as a symbol of abundance, or on desk to create Qi flow. Clean windows, computer screen, and mirrors because they are a water element. Do not use fresh flowers in bedroom because they create too much yang energy and disrupt sleep, do not use dried flowers, because they have no Qi.

BALANCE

Feng Shui is an art and science of principles derived from ancient Eastern practices that is designed to balance and harmonise the home or workplace which in turn creates balance and harmony within oneself. If one's home is healthy, then the individual can be healthy, in mind and body. This also assists with better insight to make the right decision, especially when you are torn between opposing situations, ideas, or people as well as help in resolving conflicts between people or to keep conflicts from escalating. When balance or yin and yang is achieved in the environment a positive energy flow is created. There are many factors in an environment that can block this positive flow of energy, and one aspect is organisation.

Yin and yang are defined as two halves that together complete wholeness. When something is split or incomplete, it upsets the equilibrium of wholeness. This starts both halves chasing after each other as they seek a new balance with each other. Yang means "sunny or bright", and corresponds to the day and more active functions. Whereas yin, means "shady or dark", and corresponds to night and less active functions. These opposites are polarity required for harmonic balance. Opposing or contrary forces are complementary, interconnected, and interdependent in the natural world, and how they give rise to each other as they interrelate to one another. Duality exists in everything whether tangible or intangible, some examples are hot/cold, tall/short, or male/female. Duality is found in all and are parts of Oneness

Yang energy: white, heaven, male, active, day, sun, contraction, mountains, light colours, loud music, round shapes and round people, optimistic, energetic, young, outside and active.

Yin energy: black, earth, female, receptive, night, moon, expansion, valley, dark colours, silence or soft music, long shapes and tall people, pessimistic, exhausted, old, inside and passive.

When your life is out of balance, analyse the balance in your home and workplace. Balance the Five Elements: fire, water, wood, earth and metal. Also add air to the spaces. Each of these elements works independently and collectively to restore calm and bring energy to your space. Balance and harmony is imperative in Feng Shui practice, it is recommended that a Feng Shui Consultant is appointed to ensure this is created to its optimum level. However, below is a starter.

Earth – Earthy colour tones. Crystals or clay.

Metal – Silver or gold

Water – Blues. Water or glass.

Wood – Greens or browns. Timbers or plants.

Fire – Fiery colour tones. Sun or candles.

Create harmony for a stronger connection between who you are and what you do, to increase peace and harmony in your life as well as reduce the conflict, drama, and stress in your home or workplace. Create this in your landscape, home and workplace. To do this the five elements – wood, fire, earth, metal, and water – must be in harmony in each room/space.

When an element is not represented in an area, place something of that element. For instance, missing the wood element, place something to represent wood. When an element is overpowering, weaken it with the appropriate element from the weakening cycle. For example, an overpowering timber room, place fire elements such as reds or candles in the space for balance. When one element creates a lot of chaos, clash, or disaster, repaint the room.

Use the elements listed below in various combinations, enhance, weaken, or control your spaces. Ensure all of the elements are represented in each space.

Productive Cycle:
WOOD fuels FIRE
FIRE creates EARTH
EARTH produces METAL
METAL condenses or holds WATER
WATER feeds WOOD

Weakening Cycle:
WOOD reduces WATER
WATER reduces METAL
METAL reduces EARTH
EARTH reduces FIRE
FIRE reduces WOOD

Destructive Cycle:
WOOD consumes EARTH
EARTH dams WATER
WATER extinguishes FIRE
FIRE melts METAL
METAL cuts WOOD

Wood harnesses the power of creativity and expansion. Wood also represents birth, strength, flexibility and intuition. There must be proper balance in the use of wood in your space as too much creates overwhelment, stubbornness and inflexibility. Not enough wood creates lack of creativity, indecision and depression. Place plants, paper, furniture or textiles. .

Fire increases enthusiasm and leadership skill. In the home fire is used to encourage expressiveness, inspiration and boldness. With fire a perfect balance is essential. Too much fire creates anger, aggression, irritability and impulsive behaviour. A lack of fire creates emotional coldness, lack of vision, inexpressiveness and low self-esteem. Place some candles, electronics or natural sunlight.

Earth affects our physical strength. It creates grounding, balance and stability. An overabundance of earth in a space, creates a sensation of boredom, sluggishness and seriousness. Too little earth creates disorganisation, chaos and lack of focus. Place images of landscapes or square shapes. Do not place images such as snowy mountains.

Metal affects mental clarity and logic. It creates organisation, focus, righteousness and analytical abilities. Too much metal creates chattiness, overly critical thoughts and speaking without thinking. Too little metal creates cautiousness and lack of focus. Place items of iron, aluminium, gold or silver;

Water responds to spirituality and emotion. A balance of water creates inspiration, wisdom and insightfulness. Too much creates feelings of unbalanced growth and the sense of emotionally drowning. It can make you feel overwhelmed and overly social. Too little water creates lack of sympathy, loneliness, isolation, and stress. Try incorporating water into your space by adding blacks, blues or reflective surfaces.

Quick tips

Connect to your space personally to empower your life. Display your favourite art or patterns you love to help forge a strong bond between you and your environment.

In order to make a room look and feel magnificent, you must think about adding gravity and balance to the space. Think about your home or workspace as a living, breathing entity that wants to feel the same. A bare dining or coffee table with art on the walls feels very different to a table that has a centrepiece displayed. This centrepiece creates visual focus that organises the room in a new way, helping it to appear more settled.

Open space welcomes new opportunities and gives relationships room to flourish and thrive. Clear space for happy conversations. By removing non-essential excess, it allows the flow for comfort and nestled joy.

Display symbols that represent wealth to you.

Open your windows wide and often, and replace recycled air with a fresh Qi. Place live plant, this purifies air and keeps the energy in your space vibrant and wealth-ready.

Activate your Home or Office For Success and Money

Invite guests over and feed them this indicates you are abundant enough to feed many mouths, you generate a prosperous energy and like energy attracts more like energy. This also enhances happiness in your space.

Appreciate the true abundance in your relationships and space. When you practice appreciation in your environment, all those who come into your space feel love. When we notice and show gratitude for what is good in our life, it amplifies a trail for more success to your life.

Change your home or workspace by giving it beauty and order, and it will fill with purpose and clarity. Life imitates our environments, show and act with love daily and the big things you desire manifest more easily. When positive experiences occur around you, give thanks. This is a sign that more good things are on their way.

Life is divided into nine fields: prosperity, fame and reputation, relationships and love, creativity and children, skills and wisdom, helpful people and travel, career, family, and health. Analyse Your Qi Flow and Determine which areas in your life need the most work and a greater flow.

Keep things clean and organised.

When someone compliments you, thank them and let them know how happy it makes you.

Go out dancing and celebrate.

In your relationships, your task is to create harmony in your family, wherever they are.

Be spontaneous and creative.

Take enough time to enjoy people.

To have a great relationship with yourself, take a meditation class or listen to a guided meditation

Be mindful of your boundaries. Help and mentor people but ensure you have boundaries, without them you will lose yourself in the relationship.

See your health and relationships as your greatest wealth and abundance.

Build strong bonds with your loved ones and colleagues.

Activate your Home or Office For Success and Money

To avoid games and drama in your life, avoid any kind of games, such as video games or board games, in the east and southwest of your home.

Bamboo is considered to be a symbol of good luck, place this in your lounge room or workspace.

To ensure the flow of Qi does not rush upstairs or down, place a plant or another focal point at the side of the staircase, not bright red or close off the stairs with a door or screen.

Do not leave wastebaskets, clutter, or dirt in any direction that you activate.

Activate General Directions, in lounge room, workspace and bedrooms unless otherwise stated – pertaining the connected direction.

Do not place dried flowers, the positive Qi no longer exists in these.

Many have discovered the benefits of Feng Shui. If you would like to invite more success and money into your life, begin with these principles and expand the energy in your home or workspace. In the eastern culture, those who find success through Feng Shui practises do not sell their homes once they become millionaires. They keep it for luck and continued good energy, even if they move into a new house.

Everything we do is controlled by the energy we put into it. Feng Shui helps release stagnated energy and escorts in good energy. Those who find the right balance in their homes discover that when the right energy is in place their success increases. Feng Shui is an ancient science and art that many people have had success with, and it's possible for you to have that same success, as well

For complete and comprehensive balancing, activations and cures for your home or workspace, contact a Feng Shui Consultant. Please note: Direction identification with a compass is the only way to get an accurate reading of your environment. More than half of the people who conduct their own Feng Shui compass readings do it incorrectly. It's imperative that it's accurate; creating analyses based on inaccurate readings is worse than doing nothing to correct or remedy inauspicious elements in your home.

Create a Vision board

A vision board is a paper or board where you put in the centre a recent image of yourself in a professional outfit, what a professional outfit is to you. Place images around it that represent Success and Money to you. Place your vision board in the southeast direction in your workspace

The Power of YOU

Your space is unique, just like you are. Learn to listen and cooperate with it. Your environment is showing you the evidence of your results as well as your thought patterns. Feng shui is there to help support your efforts, and not replace them. You are capable of anything you choose and put your mind to. You can transform your life to anything you desire. Match the frequency and you get exactly that, like attracts like. The following are statements to help you know you have the power;

Becoming prosperous is not a matter of what environment you start in, it is a matter of causation. Things come to you when you make them come to you.

Do not accept there is no way for you to make money, just remember the world as well as the universe has endless resources.

Everything we use, live in or entertain ourselves with is as a result of an initial thought, thoughts always find a way to manifest into reality. Have a clear thought of the end result. Get in the mindset of dedication and that you are a successful person and that is what you will be. It is not enough to have a general yearning for wealth and success, many want this, what you need it a specific goal, exactly how much do you want to be earning in one years' time? Exactly what do you want to be doing in one years' time? This is what you need to answer. Write with a purpose and point. It is specific aims that will come true and general aims that will not. Keep your desire in mind. Have a destination in mind, never sway from that compass and continue to move toward it. Once you have a thought live it, breath it and it will soon be a reality. The power to turn thoughts into success lies in the ability to control the way that you think. Thinking health in the midst of disease and thinking wealth in the midst of poverty is the key to success. Do not become distracted by other people's failure or they will become your own. Don't think according to what surrounds you or you have no control over your fate.

Invite wealth by considering others. You should want for others what you want for yourself and wealth will come to both of you.

Map your goals
Determine your personal and professional goals to ensure you align Feng Shui with your targets. Write them down and use blue ink, blue represents power. State your goals in the positive and specify what you want, not what you do not want. It must

be within your control decide what you want, not what you want for another. For example, the goal "I want my husband to get a better job" is not within your control; you cannot control how someone else feels or what they want. Consider, "I help create an environment that supports my husband's success, and happiness." Ensure your goals are around what you desire. Your goal must be something you value. Not what another wants you to be, do or have. Always write your goals in the now as if they are already in place this helps stimulate the flow of Qi and the universe operates in the present moment and remember to always finish your intention with "This or something better."

Activate each goal with an image that represents your intentions, however you see this goal to be.

Chinese Proverb

"He who craves wealth joins the party".

Being Gracious and Appreciation

Being Gracious and feeling appreciation are powerful processes, and both invite a tremendous flow of positive Qi that continues to amplify as this is practised daily. The next pages are simple lists of statements and things that help us feel good. Use these lists, choose your favourites, rewrite them, add to them, and play with them. Make this a daily occupation. Feel good now! And your abundance for health, success, relationships and growth will come swiftly.

99 Things You Can Be Gracious for on Any Given Day
I am gracious for...
1) Blazing orange and magenta sunsets
2) Quiet dawns in the darkness of early morning
3) Jacaranda trees
4) Exotic flowers like lilies and orchids
5) Books
6) Comfy, warm home on a cold day
7) Neon-green newborn grass emerging in spring
8) Supportive, loyal friends

9) Giving and receiving
10) Art in all its forms
11) Sparkles on the surface of water
12) Sturdy strong trees
13) Strong bodies that move us
14) Fairy lights
15) The first spring flower rising up
16) Optimism
17) Positivity
18) Silliness
19) Gratitude!
20) Indoor plumbing
21) Laughing till your tummy hurts
22) Deep emotion and passion
23) Our guides and angels
24) Turquoise
25) Walks in nature
26) A favorite song
27) Dancing madly
28) The golden light on nearby mountains
29) Doors for privacy
30) Quantum physics
31) Infinity
32) Worlds upon worlds

33) Feng Shui
34) A warm soup in winter
35) Clear deep rushing rivers
36) Jumpers and jackets
37) Baby lambs, puppies, kittens
38) Food glorious food
39) Too many bubbles in a bubble bath
40) My skin
41) Goofy faces
42) My happy family
43) Technology that connects the world
44) Pen and paper
45) Renoir, Picasso, Van Gogh
46) Pungent fragrances of lavender, rosemary, mint, rose
47) Pop Music to rock out to
48) Wisdom through the ages
49) Words like wonderful, luscious and nourish
50) Mother Teresa
51) Modern day mystics
52) Playtime especially when we are all grown up
53) Looking at the night sky
54) Comfortable bed
55) Unfurling of a fern frond
56) Water! Drinking it and knowing we are mostly made of it

57) The universal language of music
58) Yellow
59) Scurrying possums
60) The bustle and mix of animals, people, cars and bikes in Melbourne
61) Stretching our bodies
62) Hugs and kisses
63) Sharing with like-minded friends
64) The whole intricate, multi-layered systems of our bodies
65) Siblings through thick and thin
66) Loving, caring, nurturing mothers
67) Steady, sensible, hardworking fathers
68) Double rainbows
69) The wonder of birth!
70) Peace, quiet, serenity
71) Cars that transport us
72) The internet
73) The brilliant, bright extravaganza of summer
74) The vast ocean – the waves and tides and immensity
75) The magic of life
76) Scientists and mathematicians
77) Magenta
78) Routines we can count on
79) The fact that our world is spinning, and we feel stable

80) Tropical islands
81) Dancing and laughing
82) Red
83) Melodious singers
84) The beat of drums
85) Enjoying a cool salad on a hot summer day
86) Honesty and forthrightness – people you can count on
87) Exquisite rain falling
88) Blue, and all the myriad of shades of it
89) Eyes that are a window to the soul
90) Smiles
91) Love – agape love, family love, self-love
92) The feeling of joy that upwells from within
93) The Earth's incredible beauty
94) Purple
95) Other life in the universe that is undoubtedly there
96) Particles and waves dancing and disappearing
97) Confidence and Trust
98) Kind deeds and compassion
99) All the things left off this list…

NATURAL JOYS

Think about these one at a time before going on to the next one.

1. Being in love.
2. Laughing so hard your face hurts.
3. A hot shower.
4. No queues at the supermarket.
5. Taking a drive on a pretty road.
6. Hearing your favourite song on the radio.
7. Lying in bed listening to the rain outside.
8. Hot towels fresh out of the dryer.
9. Chocolate milkshake ... or vanilla ... or strawberry!
10. A bubble bath.
11. Giggling.
12. A good conversation.
13. Finding a note in your jacket from last winter.
14. Running through sprinklers.
15. Laughing for absolutely no reason at all.
16. Having someone tell you that you're beautiful.
17. Accidentally overhearing someone say something nice about you.
18. Waking up and realising you still have a few hours left to sleep.
19. Making new friends or spending time with old ones.

20. Having someone play with your hair.

21. Sweet dreams.

22. Making eye contact with a cute stranger.

23. Holding hands with someone you care about.

24. Running into an old friend and realising that some things (good or bad) never change.

25. Watching the expression on someone's face as they open a much-desired present from you.

26. Getting out of bed every morning and being grateful for another beautiful day.

27. Knowing that somebody misses you.

28. Getting a hug from someone you care about deeply.

29. Knowing you've done the right thing, no matter what other people think.

For more information about this author
And other books:
www.terminaashton.com
www.terminafengshui.com
www.perpelflame.com
www.thehappymagnet.com

www.ingramcontent.com/pod-product-compliance
Lightning Source LLC
Chambersburg PA
CBHW050439010526
44118CB00013B/1595